POEMS OF RECKONING AND HOPE

"I once was told that poetry is painting pictures with words. Felix paints entire stories with his poetry. His artistry shines through his poetry and shares a life story that is ongoing, creative and often painful….As a sociologist who appreciates narratives of the human condition, as an amateur poet who loves painting pictures with words, and as a fellow sufferer of living with chronic ailment and disability, I admire Felix's honesty and generosity. In a world where much is not right, it is a better place for having someone like Felix in it, sharing his life with all of us through his art of the language."

PATTIE THOMAS, PH.D.
Sociology professor, College of Southern Nevada
co-author of **Taking Up Space**

"Felix Garmendia is a friend whose presence in my life is a rare gift. My copy of *Flying on Invisible Wings*, the first volume of Felix's collected poems, rests on the nightstand beside my bed. I read from it nightly, and Felix's reflections on his own life—how he has met the challenges facing him with positivity, determination,

and a will to succeed—allay my personal fears
and self-doubts, enabling me to sleep peacefully
and to awaken each morning with renewed hope
for the future.

I invite everyone who needs reassurance
in these troubled times to join me in reading
his second book, *Poems of Reckoning and Hope.*

DR. DENNIS A. LICHTY
Professor of Education
Dean of Education & Counseling, Retired
Wayne State College
Wayne, Nebraska

POEMS OF RECKONING AND HOPE

FÉLIX GARMENDÍA

PEARLSONG PRESS
NASHVILLE, TN

Pearlsong Press
P.O. Box 58065 | Nashville, TN 37205
www.pearlsong.com | www.pearlsongpress.com

Purple feathers photo 201603630 © Weerayuth Kanchanacharoen;
clouds illustration 144910753 © Studiom1 | Dreamstime.com.
Liberty drawing by Bansai.
Photo credits: pp 56, 58 & back cover by Alexandra Wang;
pp 39, 78, 86, 137 by Denis Beale.

Trade paperback ISBN: 9781597190992
Ebook ISBN: 9781597191005

ALSO BY FÉLIX GARMENDÍA
Flying On Invisible Wings

Library of Congress Cataloging-in-Publication Data

Names: Garmendía, Félix, 1961– author.
Title: Poems of reckoning and hope / Félix Garmendía.
Description: Nashville, TN : Pearlsong Press, [2022] | Summary: "In his
    second book of poems, Félix Garmendía has settled into New York
    City's Washington Heights with his husband, Denis. There he bears
    witness to and chronicles the frightening events of recent years—
    the explosion of racism, the Covid-19 pandemic, the storming of
    the nation's capitol—and shares his oases of hope"—Provided by
    publisher.
Identifiers: LCCN 2021057179 (print) | LCCN 2021057180 (ebook) |
    ISBN 9781597190992 (trade paperback) | ISBN 9781597191005
    (ebook)
Subjects: LCGFT: Poetry.
Classification: LCC PS3607.A755 P64 2022 (print) | LCC PS3607.
    A755 (ebook) | DDC 811/.6—dc23
LC record available at https://lccn.loc.gov/2021057179
LC ebook record available at https://lccn.loc.gov/2021057180

To my husband, Denis,
because within the corners of my time
only you can deflect fate.

INTRODUCTION

Félix's first book of poems, *Flying On Invisible Wings,* encompasses a journey from Puerto Rico to New York, a journey from his discovery of being gay to a deeper understanding of himself as he lives and experiences the splendors and difficulties of life as a gay man in Manhattan. These include marches in pride parades, exploring intimacy, surviving AIDS, finding love and marrying, living with Inclusion Body Myositis.

In his second book, we meet Félix as he shows us his now-home ground of Washington Heights and comes to know it and celebrate it. However, we also travel with Félix deep into troubled America during the era of Trump: its racism, its disinformation, its hatred of many different groups of people, its homophobia.

We are also privileged to read about Félix's deep, loving and sometimes up-and-down relationship with his husband, Denis. And of its amusing moments, as well. Then the pandemic hits, and Felix speaks of it in poetry as no other poet can, in loving, ironic, searing detail. He also writes of the horror of the Capitol Riot and break-in, and of the sorrow we experience as Black men die at the hands of White police.

Yet in the midst of these nation-battering and changing events, he is able to locate humor and bring hope into our lives through the poems in the last two sections of the book.

As we flew with Félix in his first book, we now ride into the heart of the storm, into the depths of passion, sadness, recklessness and redemption.

And in the midst of it all, he and his poems remain incomparable, enduring, unforgettable.

FRANNIE ZELLMAN
M.A. creative writing
Editor of & contributor to the **Fat Poets Speak** *series*

Within the isolation of the pandemic, I grew fond of my immediate world. In our old apartment in Washington Heights I share my space, my time, my whole flawed persona with my husband, Denis. His presence keeps me sane as we shelter from the storm of Covid.

In disbelief, we watched the riots of January the 6th. I watched bigots break down doors and run down the halls armed with weapons, Confederate flags, words of hate and screams of delusional supremacy over the will of the people.

But no storm lives forever. Those who desecrated the idea on which a nation was built will be prosecuted.

I therefore proclaim a new reality. As a nation we are waking up to injustices which prevailed over the small minds of those who wanted to turn back time.

The newer generations will crown with olive

branches the only god I recognize, peace of mind. Hope in my American journey becomes me. From these different landscapes I have composed a series of poems that I offer to you in this second book.

Let us go through the heart of the storm and out of it together.

Félix Garmendía

CONTENTS

IV Poems of Play, Reverence and Irreverence

I
THE
RECKONING

Harvest of Time

I think death is scared of me.

AIDS:
I witness pines in the forest fall
ignited by indifference:
misinformation,
mass panic,
brush fire leaves a desert behind.
And I still stand
in the middle of the traffic
of those
leaving before me.

2001:
Inclusion Body Myositis
snaps branches,
frightens my roots:
legs,
left arm
paralyzed.
A wheelchair
stops footprints,
leaving
tracks
where hope
dwells underground.
I remember this melody.
I sing shadows away
one more time.

2020:
Rooted on this earth,
cheating decades
of their darting
unsuccessful
rain of
crossbows.
I plant tomorrows as I go.

America's Ninth Life

Not everything can be kittycats playing with yarn.
But I still like to see them in the pet shop window
    on 181st street.
They are oblivious to the complications outside
    the store window.
Lindsey Graham's rabid thoughts:
He must not believe in vaccines.
Coronavirus panic:
Trump claims everything is under control.
Gun violence, global warming:
The right wing doesn't see the point.
Hate crimes rocketing.
At risk: Liberty and justice for all.
I've forgotten
the joy of not living afraid at home.

America breathes denial,
sleeping through its crisis.
Like an old cat
that forgot the simple joys of yarn.

ANOTHER FALL

Félix counts
all
the time.
Preceding 60.
Glides
a second short
of the next minute,

wondering
how many broken tailed comets
will regrow light.
Remembers
Grandma›s garden.
His many failed attempts
to merge.
The plane to New York—
Recalls
pressing
one row
of flower petals.
Blown Murano glass unicorn,
fields of skulls.

Heart
of the forest
where
he once learned
that leaves
rest silent

and peace
falls
slow.

AUTUMN DURING THE PANDEMIC

Night in Washington Heights.
Leaves about
to become root food.
The colder winds
return
every evening.
Red,
orange,
yellow,
brown
and branches
now leafless
in Fort Tryon Park.
The river will freeze,
but not quite yet.
Autumn engages
the night
and the masked
friends
who have been gay
forever,
like me.

The street dances
become slower.

AUTUMNAL

In 15 minutes,
it will rain.
I watch
the dark clouds
spread
shadows
through
a dusty window
I'll never clean.
The dry earth
will be glad.
The pavement will shine.
The flame-colored leaves
will fall faster
to the ground
by the weight
of rain over mist.
An old Gregorian chant
will ride the fog
over Fort Tryon Park.

My chest
sinks
in the dense silence
strangling
my veins.
Earth will burn,
then die again.
This time

FÉLIX GARMENDÍA

I wonder if there
will be
another
spring.
I'm tired.
Time to rest?
It just started to rain.

BLINK

Birds migrate to escape the frozen clouds.
Cornucopia of minutes feeds the hours,
days and nights arrest: light blink of a galaxy.
Life stutters, then reclaims.

BURNING LEAVES

In orange sky, yellow mounts red in angry bolt.
Spirits give birth to comets, borrowing warmth
      from red.
Burned leaves, embers die into fire before becoming
      fire again.
Heat of suns, earth harvest, quasars of the equinox.
Then chill.

I can feel the air and it hurts.

Closer

I shroud my body in the music of new senses.
A sudden speck of light in a shower of stars.
A loose pearl mixed in the sands of the departed.
A memory of jasmine from a child.
A new return to the indestructible
in another space in a different time.
I count my earth time in lifespan of roses.

I move closer to returning to the forest of celestial
    bodies
where time is counted in the spirits of sequoias.

Dinner in the Time of the Apocalypse

Blue and gold jacket,
avoiding
lunch
to devour
supper.

An attitude
of
"everything feels normal,"
after shackled
days,
fear of breathing.

Pearls
mimicking their
unveiling
after
being too
long in a shell.

Tonight
I'm getting drunk
because I can.

Closing Ceremonies

My body finds frontiers.
Accelerating the process of changing my form,
I remain, satisfied with life's banquet.
My life wears the colors of famine, but still hungers
for the raw pulse of living.

ETERNITIES

My friends crawl out of their caskets at sundown.
Open-eyed thirsty shadows
submerged in night,
they roam the streets
after New Amsterdam created
the webbed winged presence
from above.
Camouflaged,
engulfed in black clouds
embroidered with midnight.
They live
the human need
to own eternity.

Eyes

Worried eyes behind the masks.
An unwanted carnival
spreading panic
we all attend,
covered.
No smiles.
Just dilated pupils
submerged in a thick twilight we can't stop.
Young eyes,
adolescent eyes,
adult eyes,
old eyes.
Sadness.
Empty stares.
Icy galaxies.
Eyes that bleed loneliness in quiet.

As a tree hurts.

FAGulous

I decorate my skin with jewels
to ride Pegasus
and sit
in front of the computer.
Getting ready for a conference call,
after 8 pm
as I look at the image
on my bronze cherub mirror
and rejoice.
On my game—
a silk shirt,
sapphire and diamond earrings,
necklaces,
no pants,
no need for the illusion.
An open shirt—
pierced nipples glare
18K gold rings,
one in the shape of a penis,
the other with a diamond.
Tennis bracelet,
17-carat ruby ring
surrounded by a halo
of 40 diamonds.

Dressed
for nobody but
me and my two friends
on a slow

Covid-19
evening.

Fangs

My heart beats famine,
centuries become a
life sentence.
I sprout skin-webbed wings
in the shadows of human fear.
Through the scent of death interrupted
I thrive.
Over lifetimes
I puncture
trails of lust
quenched until the sun dies.

Fear and Resurrection

The night after my first
20-plus years in the closet,
breathing fear from my darkness,
I come out hungry for living.
Breaking the suspended bubble of lies
I dive into the pool of newly awakened flesh,
hungry wolfman skin,
carnivore for man meat.

But I am hunted early
by the crossbow of fate's betrayal.
1989—
HIV.
My calendar shrinks
like a dying poisoned tree.
The calendar cutters don't count
on the depth of my roots.
Other trees fall next to me,
some of them over my wood arms.
And I remain
like an old story,
unfinished,
condemned to tell.

Félix in the Time of Pandemic

I might just ask to wear jewelry,
look at myself in the mirror, gleam,
and just puff Covid away.

I am a poem on two chicken legs.
I do not contain multitudes.

But I can crow lustily
For my dinner.

Félix Vampire

Accomplice of a lusty moon.
Un-miracle of nature by night, vampire of words
    by day
in a world of wounded humans, quenching thirst on
    broken souls.
Fangs search where mirrors scream for a face.
Flying
I embrace myself in the darkness of the bite.
Snatched away from the sun,
sinking my teeth one more night in the undead.

I wake in the casket of my open eyes.

In Spite (Inclusion Body Myositis 2)

I push what I know as time to the frontiers of my
    skin, I celebrate phantom days for obscure
    reasons and forget others to avoid the
    sundown.
I crystalize under pressure and facet after the
    pruning of sleepless nights. Thinking about
    tomorrows I live my days fiercely.
I feed on light and sweat the gleam to guide my
    steps. In todays, I shine brightly.
Time in me has proven itself immeasurable, like the
    number of alien souls wandering among stars.
An illusion of petals or feathers on peony swans.
A visceral presence of blood in Goya's "Third of
    May, 1808."
I keep opening my eyes to a familiar space where
    comfort and safety rival oxygen for my
    survival.
I challenge time with millions of origami doves that
    circle forever my Venice memories.
I build a home with a swirl of yesterdays pointed at
    the living of each today.
I find him in the crowds of men my arms tasted.
Below the shadows and dust of an old masterpiece's
    frame, I bury death sentences, toxic darkness
    and suspended dreams.
In me today and every day after fractures the DNA
    of human measured time.

I am ahead of it, because I have lived long enough
to see old suspended dreams sprout from
forgotten corners.

In the Closet

Nothing grows
in the dark.
Eternal hibernation.
Fossilized
dry
static,
feasting on shadows
sweaty damped walls,
self-caged canary

afraid of flying.

INERTIA

Inertia: dried-out blood on sizzling skin.
We hunt our own, over and over again. The bull's
        eye that targets the different,
the children,
the devoted,
those massacred by the trigger of hate.
The grim reaper draped on 50 agonizing stars;
his black cloak erases the last steps of those who
        couldn't escape.
In the name of supremacy
we, once the land of new beginnings, close our
        eyelids.

America, are you scared of looking or dying? Or
        living?

Into the Wind

I open my hawk eyes to the light once again,
unsure of the best time to spread my feathered
      arms and rise above the somber smell of
      withered blossoms.
The skies are old pewter, weighing over my head,
      like my survivor guilt.
I've lived a death sentence for 30 years now, but my
      skin refuses to dry out and fly away.
I still see feathered friends leaving too soon; the
      world chooses to forget.
Today the walls are walking towards me. I feel the
      heaviness that weighs down my wings.
I cannot rise above my land or separate myself from
      the thoughts of confused ravens flying into
      the wind.

Joy

I, Capistrano swallow that refused to return. Snail
in the night leaving a gem-studded glow trail
for someone to find their way in the night.
Scribble on a napkin of a starving artist, Keith
Haring subway graffiti under layers of time.
Once hidden now bathing in sunlight, damaged
goods to surviving medieval unicorn tapestry:
survivor.
I find my ground, I root identity, goals and hope of
growing old in spite of rapidly decaying flesh.
Escaping shadows, forgotten negatives of old
pictures in a dusty old shoe box.
I am hypnotized by the spark.
I live in the reality of the ephemeral rose.

KNOCKING ON ALLEN'S GRAVE

I need a new body and a nice bite for eternity.

I desire to be bitten by Ginsburg (Allen, that is),
let myself bleed down his throat.
And kiss his fangs,
finding in his entrails
the birthplace
of my next verse.
Fuel for another line
to extend my stay.

Mabon's Twilight

I dance in a way I never did to a music sung by
    newly born sirens.
I leave behind my chair where forgotten cricket
    songs morph into warm colored leaves.
In the fall, I sing maroon ballads in daylight and
    hum whale hypnotic chords to greet the dusk.
I travel hidden roads on Hermes's borrowed winged
    sandals.
I tree, remembering how to let go.
Solace: one more year in the autumn of Fort Tryon
    Park.

ON THE CUSP

Félix Garmendía,
we are just an accident!
Something that from day one,
dies every day a little,
and almost didn't happen.
Becoming the elder star with counted time.
The short-lived firefly,
the untold truth.
We summon moon and steal light
and kidnap happiness if needed.
We can't wait for Prometheus to bring us the fire.
We char more than time with our desires.
Most vegetate between realities.
A few end the phrase "I am…"

So—why the hurry?

One Day

My body refracts in shadows,
I plant seeds in the cracks of dead dirt. Thirsty for
      yesterday's memories, though they are
      unavailable when illness strikes.
Maybe one day, a seed I gave up on will decide to
      sprout and bloom in blood.

Is it time?

PITCH BLACK

The night is slow and dense like a mass of tar, a
    piece of apache tear obsidian.
At times it becomes unbearably long, like the
    memories of a persecuted slave.
Poets' hands compose the night; they grow and
    bloom at 2 am.
Midnight flowers perfume the dance of the dead in
    forgotten built-over burial grounds.
I watch centaurs mating with the magic of a sky
    bursting with eyes of sour light.
I dream the dreams of Quixote in the eternal image
    of Elizabeth Taylor's eyes.
Dressed in black, I lurk in nightmare halls, armed
    with a beam from every finger like a wolverine.
I ride a condor to safe grounds.
Dreamland, unexpected pleasures.
I walk, I jump in enormous leaps like a scared
    gazelle escaping a king cat.
I fly like Frida after damaged legs stapled her to the
    ground.
I dance like Josephine Baker, with her talent in exile,
    words in a second language.
I am Garbo in *Queen Christina*. Silver screen in the
    golden age of Hollywood.

Time to turn the TV off and enter the twilight zone.
I remember to say hello to and embrace those long
    gone now come to play.

Buenas noches, insomniac New York.

Quarantined

Time grows a beard.
It takes a rest.
Its watch battery is dying.
Ideas jump out like dolphins
only to return before they breathe.

Sand connects the sun line.
Day wakes up night.

Nocturnal creatures dictate the last verse.

READING ABOUT LARRY
TO THE MEMORY OF LARRY KRAMER

The normal heart rests quietly
like the black hole.
A dead proud man leaves behind
his star.
Kvetch who annoyed thousands,
angered more,
but powered ACT-UP
so we wouldn't drown
in silence.
Founder of
Gay Men's Health Crisis
in the '80s,
beginnings
of the longest nightmare
from which
most never woke.
His voice:
a thunder in the night.
A bellow against ignorance, arrogance.

Someone somehow somewhere
will mate hope with echoes
as kvetchy and angry
as yours.
Thank you.

SILENT DEPARTURES

There is one thing I don't like to hear from my
    mouth or pen.
I resent it feeding on my tomorrows.
1980s, 1990s.
Past puzzles that make me go back, looking for
    missing pieces.
Pride flags with red blood spilled over the other five
    colors.
Broken soul links that AIDS, humans, and their
    time locked into the darkness of coffins.
I count the men who once studded Christopher
    Street, today a dream I write in my own HIV-
    positive blood.
Repeated phone calls to friends, dozens of
    disconnected lines.
Goodbye messages by family members, or nothing
    at all.
Friends evaporated, gone like god's reasoning under
    the lamp of logic.
Death, the terminal machete's strike that cuts the
    candle's wick.
A once-fear of mine before having my eyes stained
    by it.
I become clumsy in words, flooded with spilled
    grief.

I talked too loud, my brain resents the things that
    can't be unseen or unheard.
I, a survivor, remember too many songs I can't hum

with one throat clogged with syncopated
goodbyes.

Sirens

At a past-middle-age moment,
I sit in my wheelchair
looking forward.
The stepped-on roads call.

I stopped listening to sirens long ago.

Suspended

It's one of those days so boring you want to press
    Fast Forward.
Time slides down the bark of trees,
lava layers plant an island.
The earth entrails crystalize an opal.
A generation grows old.
And a river somewhere starts to carve a canyon.
Days like this last longer than 10 winters.
Layers of dust over inanimate objects.
The rain doesn't help—
it exacerbates the grey that tints all oxygen.
A day that forces me to think,
and I step on the book that records my life
pressing memories together,
pinching nerves that I release by flying away as high
    as I can.
Avoiding a close encounter with the sun,
an ancestral memory warns me about my wings.

THE BUST

I pose in Gioconda fashion
on a boring Covid afternoon,
my bedroom as background.
Nothing below the shirt needed.
Was Mona covered?
Keep it above the waist
to keep it safe.
Coco Chanel's wisdom in disguise.
"Don't be like the rest of them, darling."

THE STRANGEST FRUIT

You lip sync "Strange Fruit" while cooking for me.
You turn around
and tell me,
"If you were a woman, you would have been Billie
      Holiday."

We both know.
We struggle with addiction demons on our backs.

23 years after.

We've fought free.

But trees still watch
the killings.
The red pavement
where the flies
      gather.
Before the puddle
      dries.

Justice still
gets shot in the back.

TRANSCEND

"She is a fucking dude
I don't recognize!"

"He is family.
He needs your love now.
It's a matter
of his life or his death."

"Does he have a right to pursue happiness?"

"He's building over his scarred land.
He doesn't hate himself or his body now."

"I can't accept him."

"Think about it.
You loved her once.
Let him enter
your mind and heart."

How can you
specify forms
or shapes of love?
Pin them down
to bodies?

He has said
he will love.

Will he love the dude?

II
A COUPLE
OF CATS
FROM
THE HEIGHTS

HEP CATS FROM THE HEIGHTS

Both rescues,
we curl up in bed.
Most of the day
I like to look at the aquarium.
Denis shreds toilet paper.
I eat my dry food, Denis likes his soupy human stew
        canned delight.
When it comes to toys,
we are territorial.
I am faithful to my feather string.
Denis prefers to throw things down from the
        shelves.
We both stare at birdies
from the ledge of our human's living room window
facing Cabrini Boulevard.
I make bird sounds.
Denis remains silent.
Denis is a Maine Coon.
I am a Siamese.

Félix and Denis—
two contented old cats
from Washington Heights.

58 Lives

1989.
I grow deeper roots into my living pulse
as friends die of AIDS.
I learn, like a cha-cha queen, to order death around.
How many ways to celebrate life?
New lovers. Flying higher than a condor on pot.

1996.
Spared by a doctor, who goes
beyond all duty to cure me
with new miraculous meds.
Humbled by fright and amazement,
I grow new lives.

2012.
I marry and accrue blessings.
Myositis decrees that I
gain a new friend,
wheelchair called Purple Raven.
Fort Tryon Park and my new husband Denis
care for me.

2019.
My time-impaired brain exhales survival smoke.
I float in purple skies, where 58 quasars and
        planetoids mate without combat.
I have not forgotten.
They celebrate with me, those I once knew,
my gems in the constant present,

and he, my husband, who remains the brightest
and still helps me

add pages.

22 Years Ago

22 years ago, I saw you floating in an image on the
     web of lonely souls.
I remember going to bed that night with a fog of
     melodies dancing on my heavy chest.
I think I recognized you from a time swallowed by
     universes.
On February the 10th, 2012, we wove 22 years of
     life together to the Bronx clerk's office.
Happy 7th wedding anniversary to you, my love.

About Us

You are still
by my side,
against all odds,
against the prejudice,
AIDS,
hate crimes,
and the unstoppable galloping of time.
Like the face that merges
in the beveled corner of an old mirror.

Him

Mining color for your smile, plowing the earth to
  find the greens and blues of your eyes.
Sculpting in jasper for your flesh. The forests of jet-
  black wild ivy covering your chest.
The forging of iron to build the strength of your
  legs.
You are trumpet announcing lust.

Unassuming, not knowing, I hum darkness, your
  absence.

Your silver back crowned by shoulders of carbon
  under pressure.
Rothko sunlight yellow wit.
The bassoon of your voice.
Chords of morning breaking its glassiness.

You are the masterpiece I own.

I'VE LEARNED HIM

By the cadence of the keys I can tell he's reading his
      emails.
I filter the sounds of his existence through my skin.
23 years together, by now I harmonize with his
      song.
I recognize his heartbeat in the middle of a storm of
      drums.
The lyrics of his body, a Gregorian chant among
      symphonies.
His silence, my cage.
His happiness, my highest cloud.
His disappointment, my need to be better.
His sadness, my call to heal his pain.
They all recite to me the poem he is.
I respond: unfinished verse.

Suspended time holds my living thread connected
      to him.
I breathe him.
I dream him to rehearse the distance
when one of us outlives the other.

But until then, Spring is always walking towards us,
      in our land.

And time in our skin.

BODY, ART AND MIND

You are stern, like the hidden Kahlo smile.
Your enigmatic Klimt energy laces my senses with
      Burano thread.
You are a living Paul Cadmus
with the rough sensuality of a Mapplethorpe
and a melody from Caravaggio's "The Lute Player."
In your Rothko thoughts, I find the solace of an
      Andrew Wyeth landscape.
A John Singer Sargent.
Your chest, a Pollock.
Your eyes, a vibrant Matisse.
Your strength, from Michelangelo's David.
I navigate the Turner of your words in an explosion
      of light.
The solemn touch of your beliefs, a Calder-leveled
      mind.
In the sadness of a Starry Night, you offer the pink
      of an O' Keefe petal
and the yearning arms of Da Vinci's "Last Supper"
as you guide home the prismatic tomorrow of a
      Picasso.

We reside among eternities.

After My Fall

After my fall my muse is hyper,
roaming the halls
where
rust,
cobwebs,
dust
are vanquished by his hands.
He becomes dirt to grow strength,
planting roses,
overlooking another day survived.

Come, sit next to me.
Let's relax with some smoke.

As he exhales,
my healing begins.

DUNES

Around my computer,
mementos,
sands of two different worlds:
Puerto Rico and New York.
My husband cleans off layers of years in the intricate
     curves of my bronze cherub mirror.

It shines again
like the daily candle
he lights
next to me:
patches of light between the shadows,
more than dust.

AND DENIS

His ear welcomes my voice.
His eyes walk by my side looking ahead.
His hands carve music from silence
as his mind smiles and
surrounds me with colors and the light that changes
          them.
I grow there.

I call him next to me.
He is my family,
tribe.
Mine.

Or one.

Cat Among the Chickens

Poultry feeds this cat, favorite hunt.
Fried ambrosia of grease and crunch.
Denis and I breathe in crisp potatoes and chicken-
      grease scent.
They would wake hunger in a dead man.
Chickens are such delicious victims, and perhaps
in another life,
they will forgive.

The Colonel is right: I cat-lick myself.

Our Bedroom

Hats from other decades play the walls.
I watch the world spin from my wheelchair.

Shoes dance crazy minuets with silks, brocade ascots
      and bow ties.
Bronze cherubs around a gilt mirror coyly eye me.
A dusty memory of her voice sprinkles Grandma's
      Murano vases
near a rainbow bracelet from the New York
      Women's March.
A stained-glass window sports angles of red, white,
      yellow and blue; fingerprints of time.
A black iron art deco chandelier with burgundy
      tassels peers over the bed.
Blocked by the next building, a few plants twist to
      follow the light.
A jewelry box guards the marble top Victorian table.
Our eyes in the 2012 wedding picture in its '30s
      green enamel frame
wonder about this thing humans call time.

His hand protects me, caresses me:
I, old cat happy with my owner and playgrounds.

Old Photo

In a tarnished Victorian locket, pictures of two men
         in love.
A lapidary chips away, reveals the best gem
and years nurture the spirit of wine.
Patience.
Passion.
The present
grows,
blossoms
between the pages of a book.

Dry flowers decorate us.

Nest

I was independent, had an active life.
A job, many friends.
All gone but him.
That's the nature of migrant birds.
Once they limp, they must give up
the skies.

The past turned to dust, time invested in him.
Against all odds
we survived the bad weather.
I, safe in the nest he built.

Same Time, Meadow

The secret between the fox and the little prince,
      waiting for each other, every day at the same
      time, in the same meadow.
I recite routines that begin and end in you.

You dress my broken limbs.
You give me medicine.
You take me out, walk next to me in my wheelchair.

Lost in self-doubt, I find your hand—a fist of flames
      to scare away the dark.
Musical synchronicity of living. Brushstrokes.
I am the idea, you are my art.
22 years tangled up in silver: our present.
A safe land. You help me into bed.

I fly to you at night without wings.

I will not remember how to define life in your
      absence.
I will stop to meet you.

UPTOWN SLING
(OR, MRS. T WONDERS)

Denis and I build the wood frame
in the living room:
strong like the need
to finish it.
The banging of hammers
and other tools
creates a noise level
close to untenable
in our NY apartment.
Ah, but what luxurious additions:
Pillow to kneel.
Metal eagle
on the wall behind it.
Strobe light
to intensify.
Techno music
and
poppers.

Smell of new leather
and oh, yes, male sweat.
Healthy male groans
into the bargain.

Mrs, T bangs her longest broom.
"Hey, what you guys doing up there?"
she calls out the window.

"Just moving some furniture,
Mrs. T."

Right—
Isn't that what neighbors are for?

You Happen

After layers of men carved by the river of time, you
      happen.
After looking for you in ephemeral shadows, you
      pop up on a private message of a cruising
      website.
I see your pictures.
In the hot equator of a lusty hour, I run into you for
      the first time.
I become hypnotized by the forest on your chest.
Years of searching for the eye of light hidden behind
      the fog of dense cold nights.
Decades in front of open windows, waiting for our
      roots to enlace.
And it happens,
in an earth tremor of man to soul memory I
      remember your song.
Your body is new in this lifetime, your eyes echo
      timeless notes of my fingers tonight on your
      present form.
And I recall your scent tattooed on my senses,
      waking up from attempts to break the
      darkness of the night.
The one-night stands of yesterdays gone by.
The anonymous dark corner play after the closing of
      "The Eagle" and "The Spike."
The chemically enhanced devouring of bodies in
      orgies.
After all of that,
your hymn raises the flag of my now conquered skin

owned by you.
I make a million fingerprints on my body burn
       away into dead days of a past they belong to.
Our future studded with fireflies, the present
       pointing at our spark.
After 22 years, at 57, I still look at you with the eyes
       of my thirties.
We walk old familiar trails by now when we touch
       each other, herringbone of silver years.
Our aging bodies carve forever on lusty auras of
       unwritten poems.
 I crave you still with the hunger of the first time.

III
THE
RECKONING 2

TREE SPIRITS

"You can retest."

Three months.
I see it in her eyes before her voice reveals it.
She keeps on talking, my brain stops.
That green wall—
How much longer?
"A year, a year and a half—"

1989.
The words they use:
High viral loads.
Low T cells.
AZT side effects.
Brutal poison to kill the invaders.
Arms are not strong enough to stop the trees
        from falling.
Yet somehow I remain standing.

1995.
New words:
Protease inhibitors.
They fight the killers.
Body's own Star Wars.
A few trees grow back.

2020.
Coming from my regular checkup.
Do all doctors like green?
"Over 1,100 T cells."
Dr. Peter looks very happy.
The highest ever.
At this point,
still growing deeper roots,
I sit on my wheelchair,
looking forward,
thinking of the trees.

Twilight Thoughts on a Winter's Day

My child is hurting, the one inside.
But one more time, I heal him with the help of the
      spirits of Rodin sculptures,
I tickle him to happiness till he dances in lightning
      bolts of flowers.
I immerse myself in a myriad of rainbows, swaying
      to the tune of Pan over meadows of calla
      lilies.

Illness resides in this body and in millions. It has
      devastated villages and made my return to
      Venice and dreams of visiting Cuzco
      casualties of war.
But I rise above all, when the child living in me flies
      his kite high
and his laughter echoes among the clouds.

Unaware

A predator hunts
terminates a life
to keep her cubs alive.
A tree deepens its roots in the bare chest of earth.
Feeding on rain.
Overture.

A swallow migrates with a broken wing.

VOID

My mind is full of limbos tonight.
Names:
one-night stands.
Lovers.
Husbands.
Friends
I used to know
in the '80s.

We all knew where they went.

Thanks, Ronald Reagan.

WE CAN'T BREATHE

America's heart stops
when its chest
is pressed between
the tight fingers
of a fist.
Fear infects the air.

Eric Garner
and
George Floyd
couldn't breathe.
Hate
used its choke hold
and
boot,
blade over throat
to snatch away breath.
The world listens.

STOP!
Before we all suffocate.

Welcomed

From Puerto Rico,
where I was not welcome
and lived in a lightless box,
to New York
that I visited for the first time
at six.

Where I was welcome
and welcomed
at 27.

Where I am welcome
and welcomed now
at 58.

Stoned, I wake
to celebrate the
burning of
the past.

Winter from Apartment 3E

I feel the crisp breeze against the window I keep
      forgetting to clean.
White flurries fall like cherry blossom petals in
      spring
between buildings.
I have no view, but my cave is warm.
The sound of steam from old pipes in my art deco
      building
lets me know I won't go out today.

Every winter I promise I'll get the apartment
      painted.
Instead
I watch the layers of paint reveal 83 years.
Plates of time:
They fall where the humidifier mist sprays the wall
      under the old church stained glass:
maps of colors and stenciled faded flowers.

Broken Promise

We the people plant the seed of a sequoia.
But we stir a cauldron of wars.
Children caged, families separated.
"¿Mamá dónde estás?"
Some wash ashore attempting to reclaim the
      promise.
Fear, urine, sweat, feces, despair. Our own
      concentration camps.
Six deaths, infants sleep on the cold floor without
      water, food or hope.
Illness crawls under.

The tired and poor cannot breathe.
The lamp falls into the sea.

January 6, 2021

The
transfer of
power,
centuries-old
tradition.

TV blasts
terrorists
brandishing
Confederate
flags;
blue lives matter
(although they didn't).
Neo-Nazis
revisit
holocaust denial,
their hate wrapped
in the American flag.

Trump
fans the flames;
sparks of fire
spread the virus
through
thousands.

I watch
the base of democracy
cracking:

Félix Garmendía

broken glass,
mobs
screaming obscenities,
smearing feces in the halls.

And I recall with fear
my arrival
in their city.

Expose (Poem 1)

Versatile that way, like Martha Stewart.
From a high cloud
encased in its closet
god
hides
from followers,
claiming
"They wouldn't understand."
Whines:
"They recreated me in their image.
And reworded my ideas
to their convenience."
Long dispute between mortals
and eternity.

I, on the other hand,
know better
than to get
between the rock star and its groupies.

Hmm (Poem 2)

I want to take
a stroll
through Fort Tryon Park.
Nobody seems to agree.
Online
looks cloudy and cold.
Tonight must be the end
of the world.
I ask god, "Is it going to be all over in a few hours?"
God sneers,
"Mind your business, lil bitch."

Hmm.
Now who was created in whose image?

February

The
uneven
old bricks
of the next
building
settle
as
slate
dims accumulated
snow.
Shadows
press
against
the
stained-glass
window.
Trees and evergreens
from Fort Tryon Park,
now skeletal,
fade.

Another
February
in
Washington Heights.

GHOST SIGNS

I saw them often below 14th street:
Old pharmacies,
stores,
barbershops,
bars
attached to the skin of weathered bricks
deeply painted lead-paint colors.

Now they are boutiques.
We danced near them, around them,
in them.

Ghosts

The ghosts listen.
They band together inside my sleepless skin
  knowing I still crave most of them.
A planet of agonizing suns and interrupted paths.
Some of my ghosts cut out early. Others vanished
  when hope died and I needed them most.
All of them left, all forgot to say goodbye.

My ghosts dance to the lust of Camille Saint-
  Saëns—*Danse macabre,*
campfire sparks swallowed up in the dense rich
  merciless night.

HIV Survivor

Not all the horses recognize the road in the dusty
    shadows.
Some come back, unicorns mourning the last
    Pegasus in a black mass.
Others dissolve in the rain, decaying ship carcasses
    in shallow waters, stuck in indifferent mud.
Their memories, hungry hunters disturbing the blue
    stillness of my waters.
I breathe chained to millions of nameless faces,
    bodies I touch in the darkness.
I escape the crossbow shower in the shadows.
I finish the sentence of living without the ones time
    pawned into limbo.
The many names I can't start tolling. The bell
    punches breaking all silence.
The ones I remember tonight.
I restore color to my pulse, I learn to live again.

LIGHT

The afternoon shadow crawls up the next building's
        wall.
Telling me the human hour, sentence,
night over the Hudson River,
a ritual.
I wake, like a dormant seed.
Migrating
and continuing.
Taking it from where I left it

weeding.

O Say Can You Hear

My TV blasts
spilled blood.
Armed
and
brass-knuckled
insurrectionists
use
flagpoles
as weapons
to defeat the order.
I watch
the final days of
democracy:
33 years
in this
mainland
tremble.

Once I held hands
with others
demanding
human rights
in
marches
and
verses.

Chaos
explodes

while
danger
rides my breathing air.
I tremble with
lawmakers
watching
anger smear
feces on the halls
of Congress.

A loud voice
in denial
finds
all of
this
eruption
entertaining.

Some
choose
not to hear.

33 RPM and Stop

Under grey skylights
I dress in shadows,
perform a backwards waltz
to slow unsettled music:
a gramophone running out of crank.
No audience.
No curtain.
No applause.
My clumsy steps leave a
touch of cold glass,
dry cracked soil.

My monotony
melts clocks.

IV
POEMS
OF PLAY,
REVERENCE
AND
IRREVERENCE

HEAD AND BRAIN FOR SALE?
(18H)

So, husband, whose brain and head
instead of mine?

"I don't want those earrings,
I don't want those earrings."

"Yeah, Félix," he growls.
"Keep trying to convince yourself."

Elsa Lancaster's?
She
might not be interested
in writing poems.
Idris Elba, you say?
For that head I'd give
up poetry!
Spend
an eternity
looking at myself
in the mirror.

Elton John's?
Hmmm.
Is he over his larger-than-his-head
glasses period?

Husband, tell me.
Whose head should I choose?

He looks at me for a Washington Heights
minute.

Then he answers:
"Félix, do yourself a favor
and just
BUY the *!#%& earrings!"

Gargoyles Awakened

Gargoyles petrified in silver
happily leering.
A prism
drop of citrine.
Tarnished.
Black.
Wide-eyed open
from centuries.
Static
in their metal cage,
dormant,
uneasy
in what could be a tomb
inside a
jewelry box.

For sale.
Pay the price
of real flesh,
to suspend them
from each
ear lobe.

COMMUNION

My first time.
Eartha Kitt music:
"I want to be evil."
"C'est si bon."
The acid tab
hits.

We talk.
Colors get brighter.
Incense-slowed moments.
I, the NYU student, am a fairy tale prince;
Julius the counselor becomes a ballerina
Charles directs,
dressed as a king
from his ballet days,
to Elton John's
"Don't Let the Sun Go Down On Me."
Candles in hand,
I write on the air
my name in suspended neon.
We laugh,
open the window,
look at the stars,
three asteroids
that collide
on the twilight side
of the moon's
lower east side.

Leonardo

Your hands free the form from claws of matrix rock.
You tint with pigment the rose face of "Ginevra dé
     Benci."
Alpha male forms:
Your love for men walks on your palette with "St.
     John the Baptist."
Male emerges from darkness.
You leave your footprint
as you mate new kinds of love with the old
     predictable classicism.
Humanity sings. Sins?

Gioconda, are you still looking for Leonardo in the
     Louvre crowds?

CHOCOLATE
TRANSUBSTANTIATION

He comes
complete
with
chocolate
head
and crown
of thorns.
The richer
kids
from Catholic
school
sell them
for
Easter
going home
to home.
A crucifix
in
milk chocolate
with the body of
Jesus,
wrapped
in cellophane,
arms extended.
Chocolate nails
hold him to the
appetizing
cross.

FÉLIX GARMENDÍA   107

His
face,
tilted
to the side
in
suffering,
melts
under
the
Puerto Rican
sun.
Where do
you start
eating Jesus?
Like praying mantises,
most kids
start
biting
the
head off,
others the
nailed feet.
I watch them
savoring
Jesus
without
any guilt.
Training for
cannibalistic
rituals
through
delicious

transubstantiation.
Getting
ready
to
believe
when
the
bread
and wine
of communion
becomes
Christ
in
chocolate
presence.
Sorry.
I won't
eat you.
You are
grotesque.
I'd rather
take
the trip
to
Doña Sara's
candy
store
for
my
Milky Way.

I Am Félix's Beard

An ermine
around his chin.
Full and thick,
winterized
unicorn hair,
soft and long enough
to caress
like angora cat fur.
Baby goat mane.
Christmas tree
angel hair.

Once brown,
silky,
the goatee years.
Before, three hairs at the age of 11:
stooges
pointing
in different directions,
three
manic hands
of a
drowned watch.

Now, a baby butt face
with mumps
when he shaves me.

Old Pictures of Loving Men

What about those ghosts from old pictures? Where
    do they go after being trapped in time
    forever?
Where can they rest when stranger's hands go
    through them in flea market's dusty boxes?
How can they rest in solace when they have been
    separated from their loved ones, ripped apart
    like a lobotomized idea that erased the scent
    of memory itself?
I go through my affectionate men daguerreotype
    collection. And find an echo of old kindred
    soul images surviving like tumbleweeds in a
    slow sepia-scented time.
Tintypes of frozen old songs written in a forgotten
    language.
Ambrotypes of exhausted candles after lighting a
    night of lust.
Cartes de visite made to spread the magic of giving a
    present more than once.
These old ghosts sit next to each other, stare at
    others trying to undo an obvious lie.
Inquisitive in their glassy stillness. Resting on a
    silver-coated copper plate. Men in
    conservative, almost Puritan-like dress.
The old collection of pictures hides in a leather old
    Italian album, where the affectionate men
    touch each other in ways nobody dared to do.
There are dozens of glass-encased men's faces with
    furtive hands from Victorian times.

Another sleepy moment, another passion. The
    roots of green carnations bloomed wild in the
    fearful hearts of these men, escaping the
    sunlight of frowning faces and judging eyes.
These men still love each other, encased in the pages
    of my old leather album.
Please don't return them to the flea market. Give
    them to another soul who lets them vibrate in
    the flash of light that hand-printed these
    images
in forever.

GAMIN' THE SHAMAN

Shaman
and bison
dressed with
red
white
and
blue
finger-painted
face—
plastic cow horns,
raccoon tails
from
Goodwill.
Leather gloves,
bearskin cap
from yard sale,
plastic megaphone
to scream "Q SENT ME!"
Shirtless,
tattooed
over half his body,
wearing strange-
looking jeans,
he's Arizona's
poster child
for
clueless.
Jacob Chansley
flies

backwards
against the
wind.

And, out of costume,
he's something of a flat tire.

You Never Know!

It could have been a pot dream,
since we were smoking joints:
Ivan and I in our chaps, harnesses
and nipple rings
being admired by the female friend
of a movie star
while his guards were searching
frantically for him
in the Meat Packing District
on a balmy summer night
at 3 am.

And there he was, passing a joint to us,
habitues of a leather bar
out for fun
just as he was.

We heard what sounded like dozens
of feet splitting the cracked pavement,
but the man stood his ground,
toking affably.

It was only after my friend Ivan
told his female friend what a great actor he was
and she said, "Harrison, these guys are fun"
that I finally gazed
into his embattled star eyes
with the crinkles around the lids
and my jaw dropped

Félix Garmendía   *115* and he said, grinning,

"Now do you know who I am?"

10 Miles Above Oz

Violets.
Morning glories.
Lavender forget-me-nots.
Walls of pink sapphire petals
glisten in refracted light.
Glinda, don't bogart that joint!
Isn't 10 tokes enough?

Vamqueer

Good evening from the darkness
that dresses in black leather.
A whiff of their scent,
eye contact
when they pass,
veins bursting with life,
will quench my thirst.

I've walked these streets since they were New
        Amsterdam.
The hunting becomes the hunger—
I feast on willing veins.
Male furred creatures
provide my eternity.

Nice meeting you.
Would you like to walk me home?

THE BOOK OF FIRE ISLAND

Jesus dies
every year
on the clock.
It's been
32 minutes since
the
most recent
death.
He goes into
seclusion
for a long
weekend
starting Friday,
ending Sunday.
I hear
apocryphal books
tell the real story.
Where is Jesus
for three days?
The word is clear,
he escapes
to Fire Island
with his best
friend,
Mary Magdalene.
She pays for the
gas,
they take
the

Long Island
Expressway.
She wants
to visit the nude
beach and admire
bodies.
Her bronze
middle-eastern
skin
glows under the
Cherry Grove sun,
where she basks
while
Jesus
downs mojitos
at
the Ice Palace
bar.
Mary Magdalene
will meet him
there
before dinner
but after lunch.
Jesus chats
away
with the locals,
making jokes,
getting tipsy
watching
a conga line
forming at the disco.
He's cool with

two men kissing.
And two proud lesbians
with
their adopted child.

Mary Magdalene shows
up
wearing
a Hawaiian
sarong
and
they dance
till the sun
slides down.

Minutes before
Sunday,
they're
both back
in town.
Golgotha
is wondering
if he'll rise.
Jesus
orders the
earthquake,
the Roman guards
notice
the stone moving.

When Mary Magdalene
looks at Jesus's feet,

she wonders:
How in heaven's name
will he explain
the rainbow
sandals?

V
POEMS
OF
HOPE

BECOMING

Like the exit of one who meets the end of his path, I
      make room for a newly awakened sunlight.
I etch pleasure over the inside of my mirrors, like
      the breast cancer survivor plants roses over
      her scars.
I infuse flowers and pleasures. I melt what seems
      untimely with the bare truth of time itself.
I learn to weave with cloud thread my dreamcatcher.
      I honor the seconds that are the constant, the
      now becoming, in human time.

The 7 pm Washington Heights COVID-19 Yell

Residents of Washington Heights
want to be counted.
The first one screams,
"Ahooooooo."
Another,
"Helloooooooo."
Call of wolves
howling to faraway clans.
My neighbor enunciates,
"Wahooooooo,"
screech of trains
underground.
I can hear in the distance,
"Aarghhhhhh."
A second after,
fragments of songs,
whistles as loud as screeching peacocks,
even clapping out of sync,
fill with unmusical notes
an Old Faithful eruption of frustration.
Hope?

WILD GAY-ETY

Today
I officially leave my fingerprint on the chest of
      eternity.
A shower of faceted blue topaz crystals falls on my
      head and bare shoulders, celebrating life like a
      herd of thirsty elephants with a water hole in
      sight.
Today
life blooms and sprouts golden olive branches that
      remind me of triumph over a few dreams that
      met their mortality back when I no longer
      looked.
I paint a myriad of self-portraits with letters and
      tears that morph into joy over imminent
      death, spelling "Frida."
In this moment of success, I create a mural of
      repeated circles where good fortune and hard
      work crown my head.
Waterfalls sing to celebrate elation in the face of
      prior rejection.
Today
I thank the many men I pleasured and those who
      pleasured me, and the women that nurtured
      my path
with the ambrosia and nectar of wild strawberries
      and ancient harmony.

Immortality

I leave behind
an old shell
after a life
well lived,
breathing
a testament
of stubborn
will
to extend
my stay
as long as I can,
proving doctors wrong.

I reaffirm
my purpose
of living
not by actions
interrupted
by
disability and illness,
but by thoughts
printed in vital ink
that defies time.

I breathe words.

TIME IN PASSING

The terror
of that afternoon
stares
at the spilled blood,
the last
casualties
from
gusty winds
of a dying storm
it
stationed
over USA
four years ago.

Grim reapers
of
coexistence
infect
the minds of many
with a deadly virus
which
devours
brains
and
dreams.

Redemption.
The salt in the wound
of unexpected

death
burns
and
eventually
heals

passing
understanding.

II

Ruth Bader Ginsburg's
thoughts form
a lifeline,
planting
their seed.

Spring,
after
an
unfathomable
winter.
Trees survive.

I return
to Fort Tryon
Park.

The Box

Fire Island, 1997.

Cold tonight
on the Island.
I gather the logs,
open the stove.
Something inside.

You stand
behind me
smiling,
arms spread wide.
"Open it,"
you say.

New York, 2012.

We finally say "I do"
in a New York court.

Eternity
of emeralds and diamonds
finds its place
again on my finger
as it did
14 lives ago
that cold night
in Cherry Grove.

The words I need
stick in my throat.
I do not know
how "forever" sounds
in maudlin heartspeak.

The judge understands.

EL YUNQUE

Light bathes,
creates color
in impatiens,
lilies,
daisies,
parrots,
giant ferns,
bromeliads,
waterfalls.
Low sky touches your face
as fog floats over streams.
Coqui music,
pebbles,
and guppies
play with your feet.
Green lizards, butterflies,
nightingales, dragonflies
prowl, shunt over land.
Cool air.

Morning begins.

LOVERS AND OTHER GEMS

My earring enhancers:
sapphires,
rubies
versatile;
like my best lovers, I can wear them
with different gem studs.
Some are diamonds
in bed,
reflecting the string of blue
lights tangled up on my headboard.
Plastic ones?
Weak, no sparkle.
One-night stands erased.

I wear 10 emerald rings.

Amulet
against
being forgotten.

Blown Glass Unicorn

"Would you like a golden horn?"
The creature grows from melted glass,
shaping muscular equine torso:
head,
legs,
horn.
Leaping into the air,
the unicorn still gallops.
Today it is:
atoms,
air,
sound,
gravity.

Second nature.

SWIMMING WITH DOLPHINS

In a sea shack by the ocean, Key Largo humans
      gather to play with wild dolphins.
I sing under the water; dolphin gets close.
Our eyes meet, worlds without walls embracing.
Pact signed by water.

This day I read wonder in the eyes of the wild.

DEMIGODS

Dominican muscles covered with sweat glistening
    under the June sun.
Dancing merengue and salsa in the streets, on their
    way to the gym in their tank tops, shirtless on
    the lawn in Fort Tryon Park.
Washington Heights, the pulse of the Latin heart of
    New York City,
gave earth a new breed of terracotta-sculpted flesh-
    covered semi-gods.
Chests, ample like a banquet of lust.
Shoulders strong enough to hold generations of
    Latin-American pride.
Faces, creatures in a colorful rainforest, all beautiful
    in their own right.
The equators of those bodies are carved of strong
    mahogany pulsating rivers of hungry ruby
    veins.
Legs, ancient oaks like The Cloisters strong enough
    to fight the rapids of time.
I live in their forest; I am the old faun schooling
    them in how day romances the darkness of
    the night.
And I do well in their realm. Aged by wine and art,
    still driven by the flame chakra.
Red aura walking barefoot on the coals of sexual
    hunger and urge to mate.
Scorpio tattooed on my man skin. I parade the
    streets with them, tangled up in many
    summers.

I borrow a few souls by signing my name with word
or skin.

The Asgard of the male rosebuds, skin untouched
by mortality.
I watch them passing by from my 57th floor in this
forced unstoppable human time.

Exposed "New Yawk"

Félix, are you sure that
there are no crocodiles
in the sewers
of
New York City?
Do you believe that
someone ate
the big apple?
Manhattan
has been my
staff
where I
go from
classical to
reggaeton
whether
sober or stoned.
Are New York rats
the size of
capybaras?
We all know
how smart
they are, though.
Our rats
can understand
two "New Yawkas"
"tawking"
too fast
over the

noise
of subways and
screeching
tracks.
What does Félix do
on New Year›s
Eve?
Anything but
Times Square.
Too many tourists
with cameras hanging
from their necks,
in diapers quietly
peeing on themselves.
I›d rather go and
clean feces
at the Central Park Zoo!
Where does this
"New Yawka" like
to relax?
No place like Fort Tryon Park.
And, yes,
before I forget,
"New Yawk"
pizza is like
our
Streisand,
The BEST!
Are we "New Yawkas"

FÉLIX GARMENDÍA   *139*

direct?
Let me think—
is the water wet?

HARLEM I AM
TO THE MEMORY OF JAMES BALDWIN

I want to be called "Harlem"
and carry
on my shoulders
Apollo Theater—
melodies
and
African dance.
I want to walk up and down
125th street,
visit the summer flea markets,
buy Dashiki
and
Ankara fabric.

Get my goatee
groomed
in a neighborhood
barbershop.
And feed on
the spell, fragrance
of soul food,
breaking from
restaurants
and apartment
windows.

For my Caribbean ancestry
I want to be called

"Harlem."
Carved in jet
of black roses.
Stolen from Africa
now
living
in
America.

THE EMERALD THAT I WROTE

Yes, so smoking gets slower but I am cool and full of
      expectations
as I put the joint down and head to the jeweler.
Had my eyes on a ring forever.
Nobody seems to be interested.
18K yellow gold,
Colombian emerald,
diamond.
Don Pepe:
trust, excellent craftsmanship, a gentleman
of the old school, diamond district on 57th.
Younger years in Cuba:
Celia Cruz bought a large diamond ring.
He drank with Marc Antony.
His accent: a chord of Spanish guitar
that floats over English.

My happy, greedy hand
reaches, and we are both
covered in smiles. We smile in green.
A field ridiculously bright.

Transaction completed.
I wheel out of the store
with my pinky sparkling.
All from writing poems.

Somewhere it is spring in a Colombian meadow.

ENOUGH!
To the Memory of George Floyd

Our
patience
detonates,
finally.
I follow
the
process.
My
shredded
calm
pretends
to survive
Chauvin's
murderous
knee.

Today,
it flashes
on
TV:
three counts
of guilt.
President Biden and
Vice President Harris
speak.

I choose
to
let the
healing
start
from today
when
a
wounded
nation
realizes

enough
is
enough.

WALKING

For nine
years
I've wanted
to walk
as I
still
can,
in
daydreams
where
I'm granted
one
wish,
to walk
within
my
apartment,
but no further.

5 pm.
Our grandfather clock
echoes
through
the apartment.

Before nap time

just for
a fraction

of a
second,
I feel my
feet on
the ground.
As I haven't
for nine years.
I'm standing
by
myself
again.

Denis, my partner,
can't believe it.

Neither can I.

In my next dreaming
by day,
perhaps
a bird
that fell
to the ground
will heal
its wings.

ABOUT PEARLSONG PRESS

Pearlsong Press is an independent publishing company dedicated to providing books and resources that entertain while expanding perspectives on the self and the world. The company was founded by psychologist Peggy Elam, Ph.D.

FICTION

If We Were Snowflakes—YA novel by Barbara D'Souza
Heretics: A Love Story & *The Singing of Swans*—
novels about the divine feminine by Mary Saracino
Judith & *Under the Pomegranate Tree*—
historical novels by Leslie Moïse
Fatropolis—paranormal adventure by Tracey L. Thompson
The Falstaff Vampire Files, Bride of the Living Dead, Larger Than Death, Large Target, At Large & *A Ton of Trouble*—
paranormal adventure, romantic comedy & Josephine
Fuller mysteries by Lynne Murray
The Season of Lost Children—a novel by Karen Blomain
Fallen Embers & *Blowing Embers*—Books 1 & 2 of
The Embers Series, paranormal romance by Lauri J Owen
The Program & *The Fat Lady Sings*—
suspense & YA novels by Charlie Lovett
Syd Arthur—a novel by Ellen Frankel
Measure By Measure—a romantic romp with the
fabulously fat by Rebecca Fox & William Sherman
FatLand & *FatLand: The Early Days*—Books 1 & 2 of
The FatLand Trilogy by Frannie Zellman

ROMANCE NOVELS & SHORT STORIES FEATURING BIG BEAUTIFUL HEROINES

by Pat Ballard, the Queen of Rubenesque Romances:
Once Upon Another Time | *Adam & Evelyn* | *ASAP Nanny*
Dangerous Love | *The Best Man* | *Abigail's Revenge*

Dangerous Curves Ahead: Short Stories | *Wanted: One Groom*
Nobody's Perfect | *His Brother's Child* | *A Worthy Heir*
by Rebecca Brock—*The Giving Season*
& by Judy Bagshaw—*Kiss Me, Nate!* & *At Long Last, Love*

NONFICTION

Flying On Invisible Wings—poetry by Félix Garmendía
Fat Poets Speak: Voices of the Fat Poets' Society, Fat Poets
Speak 2: Living and Loving Fatly, & *Fat Poets Speak 3:*
FatDance Flying—Frannie Zellman, Ed.
Other Nations: An Animal Journal—poetry by Maria Famà
Soul Mothers' Wisdom: Seven Insights for the Single Mother
by Bette J. Freedson
Acceptable Prejudice? Fat, Rhetoric & Social Justice &
Talking Fat: Health vs. Persuasion in the War on Our Bodies
by Lonie McMichael, Ph.D.
Hiking the Pack Line: Moving from Grief to a Joyful Life
by Bonnie Shapbell
A Life Interrupted: Living with Brain Injury—
poetry by Louise Mathewson
ExtraOrdinary: An End of Life Story Without End—
memoir by Michele Tamaren & Michael Wittner
Love is the Thread: A Knitting Friendship
by Leslie Moïse, Ph.D.
10 Steps to Loving Your Body by Pat Ballard
Beyond Measure: A Memoir About Short Stature & Inner
Growth by Ellen Frankel
Taking Up Space by Pattie Thomas, Ph.D.
with Carl Wilkerson, M.B.A.
Off Kilter—a memoir by Linda C. Wisniewski
Unconventional Means: The Dream Down Under—
a spiritual travelogue by Anne Richardson Williams
Splendid Seniors: Great Lives, Great Deeds—
inspirational biographies by Jack Adler

9 781597 190992